P9-CAF-470

Pull-Out Poster Book

SCHOLASTIC INC.

New York   Toronto   London   Auckland   Sydney

No part of this publication may be reproduced in whole or in part, or stored in a retrieval system, or transmitted in any form or by any means, electronic, mechanical, photocopying, recording, or otherwise, without written permission of the publisher. For information regarding permission, write to Scholastic Inc., 555 Broadway, New York, NY 10012.

ISBN 0-590-06657-9

™ & ® & © 1997 by Lucasfilm Ltd. All rights reserved.
Published by Scholastic Inc.

12 11 10 9 8 7 6 5 4 3 2 1   7 8 9/9 0 1 2/0

Designed by Joan Ferrigno

Printed in the U.S.A.   08

First Scholastic printing, February 1997

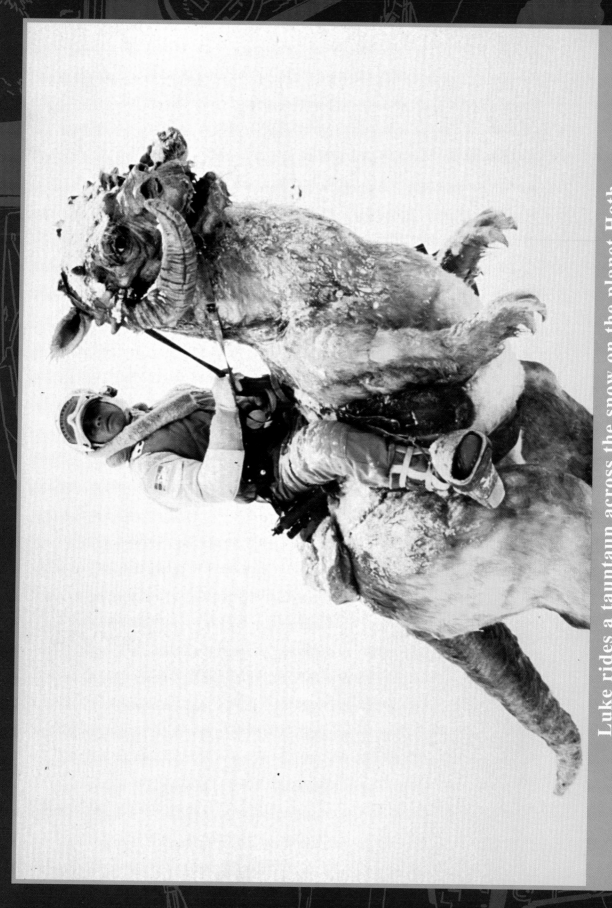

Luke rides a tauntaun across the snow on the planet Hoth.

® & © 1997 Lucasfilm Ltd.

Chewbacca scans the surface of Hoth, looking for the Imperial probe droid.

® & © 1997 Lucasfilm Ltd.

Armed with his lightsaber, Luke Skywalker learns the ways of the Jedi.

® & © 1997 Lucasfilm Ltd.

Yoda — wise Jedi Master.

® & © 1997 Lucasfilm Ltd.

"A Jedi's strength flows from the Force. But beware of the dark side."

® & © 1997 Lucasfilm Ltd.

A last-minute escape for the *Millennium Falcon!*

® & © 1997 Lucasfilm Ltd.

The Dark Lord, Darth Vader, sits in his chamber.

® & © 1997 Lucasfilm Ltd.

The *Millennium Falcon* lands at Cloud City.

® & © 1997 Lucasfilm Ltd.

Darth Vader at last reveals his secret: He is Luke's father.

® & © 1997 Lucasfilm Ltd.

Luke, Leia, R2-D2, and C-3PO watch as the *Millennium Falcon* sets off to save Han Solo.

® & © 1997 Lucasfilm Ltd.